D1709120

THE INTERNATIONAL
SPACE STATION

BY ARNOLD RINGSTAD

Published by The Child's World®
1980 Lookout Drive • Mankato, MN 56003-1705
800-599-READ • www.childsworld.com

Acknowledgments
The Child's World®: Mary Berendes, Publishing Director
Red Line Editorial: Design, editorial direction, and production
Photographs ©: NASA/Newsmakers/Getty Images, cover, 1; National Aeronautics
and Space Administration, 4, 6, 8, 10, 12, 14, 16, 18, 20, 23; Stocktrek Images/
Thinkstock, 21

ISBN 9781634074773

LCCN 2015946266

Printed in the United States of America
Mankato, MN
December, 2015
PA02280

ABOUT THE AUTHOR
Arnold Ringstad is the author of more than 30 books for kids. He loves
reading and writing about space exploration. He lives in Minnesota.

TABLE OF
CONTENTS

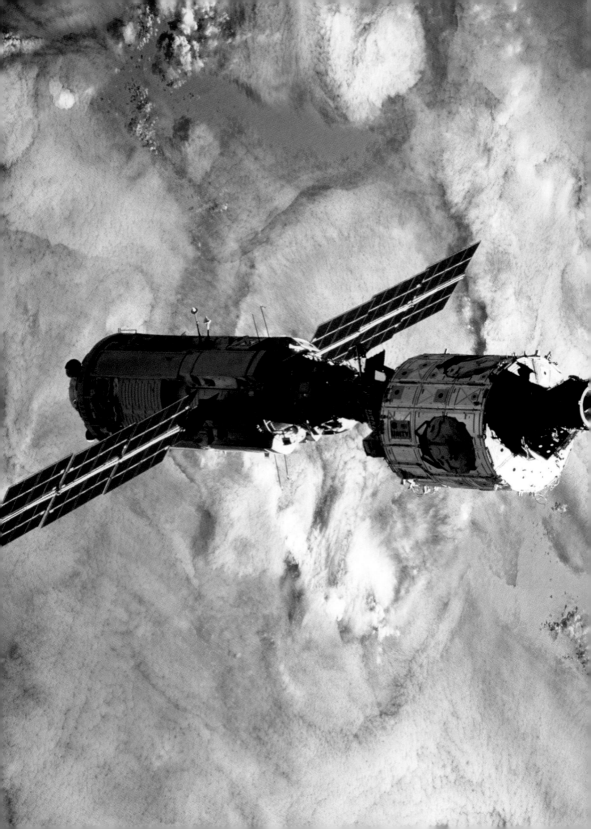

Chapter 1

THE FIRST PIECES

A voice came in over the radio: "It's time to get ready to build the International Space Station."[1] It was the morning of December 5, 1998. The crew of the U.S. space shuttle *Endeavour* received the message. They knew they had a big job ahead of them. *Endeavour* was more than 200 miles (322 km) above Earth. The shuttle zoomed around our planet. It traveled at thousands of miles per hour.

A few weeks earlier, a huge Russian rocket had blasted into space. It carried *Zarya*, the first piece of the International Space Station (ISS). *Zarya* means "sunrise" in Russian. Eventually, it would be one small piece of a huge space station. Inside the ISS, future astronauts would carry out experiments. They would learn how to live and work for long periods in **orbit**. But for now, *Zarya* drifted through space alone, miles above *Endeavour*. In its **cargo bay**, *Endeavour* carried *Unity*. This was the second piece of the ISS.

◄ The first two pieces of the International Space Station were connected in December 1998.

▲ Cabana (right) works aboard *Endeavour* with another crew member.

The job of the shuttle's six crew members was to connect *Zarya* and *Unity*. But the task would not be easy. First, the shuttle had to catch up to *Zarya*. *Endeavour*'s commander, Robert Cabana, fired his ship's **thrusters**. This pushed the shuttle toward *Zarya*. Next, the crew had to prepare *Unity* for **docking**. The doors of *Endeavour*'s huge cargo bay opened. Crew member Nancy Currie took control of the remote manipulator system

(RMS). This robotic arm in the shuttle's cargo bay let the crew grab and move objects in space.

Currie used the RMS to gently turn *Unity* upright. The **module** had been laying flat in the cargo bay. Now, it needed to be pulled out so it could dock with the shuttle. Removing *Unity* from the cargo bay was a tricky job. There was only 1 inch (2.54 cm) of space between *Unity* and the cargo bay walls. Carefully, Currie pulled out the module. She turned it over and docked it with *Endeavour*.

Now it was time to get closer to *Zarya*. Cabana fired *Endeavour*'s thrusters again. The shuttle drifted within feet of the Russian module. Currie used the RMS to grab *Zarya*. She lined it up with *Unity*'s docking port. At just the right moment, Cabana used the thrusters to push the modules together. This was supposed to connect them securely. But it didn't work. The modules were not joining together properly. If they would not connect, the mission to build the ISS might be a failure. The astronauts and ground crew scrambled to figure out what was wrong.

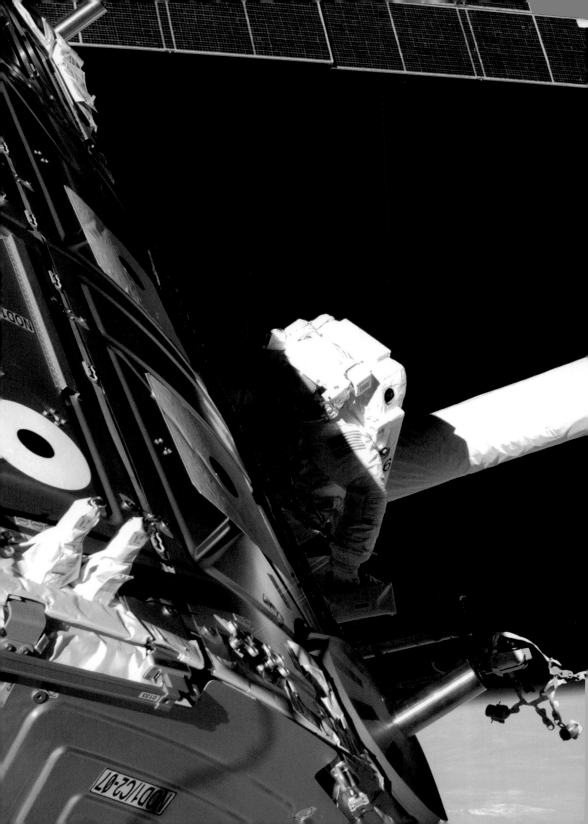

Chapter 2

PUTTING IT TOGETHER

Finally, the ground crew called the astronauts with a possible solution. They thought the gripping force of the RMS may have been preventing the modules from connecting. The arm had been holding on to *Zarya* the whole time. Currie released the arm's grip. As soon as she did, the latches on *Unity* and *Zarya* hooked together. The solution worked! The two modules locked into place, and the ISS was born.

But the astronauts could not enter the space station yet. First, cables had to be connected between the modules. This work could not be done from inside the shuttle. Two astronauts had to go into space. Jerry Ross and James Newman put on their space suits.

Ross and Newman floated out of *Endeavour* and got to work. They made 40 connections between different parts of the station. Inside the shuttle, Currie used the RMS to move the astronauts

◄ **James Newman works near the** *Unity* **module.**

▲ Astronauts perform a space walk while putting the station together.

into the right places. Ross and Newman also attached handrails to the outside of the modules. This would make work easier for future crews. After more than seven hours, the space walk was finally done. However, the pair performed two more space walks during the mission.

On December 10, it was finally time to enter the ISS. Russian **cosmonaut** Sergei Krikalev had launched aboard the shuttle with the U.S. crew. Now Krikalev joined Cabana at the hatch. The two men opened the hatch. Together, they represented the two major nations responsible for the ISS. Once inside, the pair shook hands. Krikalev floated around and did somersaults to celebrate the successful mission.

The next day, the crew returned to *Endeavour* and closed the hatch to the ISS. Later, they undocked and flew around the station. The crew took pictures and videos of it. Then, *Endeavour* returned to Earth. It touched down on a runway in Florida. The mission had lasted nearly two weeks. The ISS remained in space. It circled the globe at a height of 245 miles (395 km).

The U.S. and Russian space programs had a lot of work ahead of them. At the beginning, the station included only two modules. They planned to add at least ten more over the next several years. The first mission had involved three space walks. Planners estimated it would take at least 160 more space walks to finish building the station.

STAYING SAFE

By 2012, the ISS was nearly complete. It had several modules where astronauts could live and work. It also had huge **trusses** to hold everything together. Large **solar panels** provided electricity. Since November 2, 2000, there had always been a crew aboard the ISS. But danger lurked in orbit around Earth.

Tiny objects known as space junk circle around Earth. These items may be small pieces of used rockets. Some are pieces of broken satellites. They could even be tiny flecks of paint. Space junk travels at deadly speeds. At thousands of miles per hour, even little objects are dangerous.

Ground crews track this space junk. If a piece comes near the ISS, they warn the crew. This is what happened on March 24, 2012. The crew received a warning about a nearby piece of space junk. It was a piece of a satellite. It was left over from a satellite collision in 2009. The object was getting dangerously close to the ISS.

◀ **The nearly completed station floats above Earth.**

▲ **The Soyuz approaches the International Space Station.**

If space junk is spotted more than a day ahead of time, the station can move out of the way. But now, there was no time for a move. "It's too late," mission controllers told the astronauts aboard the ISS.[2]

The crew had to prepare for a possible strike. If the object hit the ISS, it could cause a terrible disaster. A small hit on one of the station's modules could create a hole. The astronauts' air would leak out into space. They could die.

The safest place to take shelter was in a Soyuz spacecraft. This Russian ship is used to carry crews from Earth to the ISS and back. The crew climbed into the Soyuz and closed the airtight hatch. If the debris put a hole in another part of the station, they would be safe in the sealed Soyuz. Then, they could immediately use the Soyuz to leave the station and return to Earth.

The crew waited as the space junk approached. They knew they might need to leave quickly. No one knew for sure how close the debris might fly. No one knew whether it would hit the station. They would have to wait and see.

Finally, mission controllers told the astronauts the danger had passed. The debris had passed as close as 6.8 miles (11 km). This may seem like a long distance. But space junk travels at several kilometers per second. The difference between safety and disaster can be just a few moments.

Chapter 4

LIFE ON THE STATION

It was 2009. Sandy Magnus woke up and stretched out her arms. She floated around inside her sleep pod. It looked like a small closet built into the wall. Inside was a light, a sleeping bag, and a laptop computer. Magnus opened the door. It was time to begin another day on the ISS.

Today was a weekday. This meant there was lots of work to be done. On Saturdays and Sundays, astronauts on the ISS get to relax. They watch movies and read books. They can even make phone calls to their families back on Earth. But during the week, they keep to a busy work schedule.

Magnus's first task of the day was exercise. The astronauts are always floating. Their muscles do not need to hold them up against **gravity** like on Earth. This weakens them over time. Exercise is important to keep astronauts' muscles strong.

◀ **Magnus adds a new section to a sleep pod.**

Magnus started by lifting weights. However, normal weights do not work in space. Gravity will not pull them down. Lifting them would be too easy. Instead, Magnus used a special

▲ **Magnus takes a photograph as part of her work on the space station.**

machine. It created a force for her to pull against. She also spent time on a treadmill. Straps held her against the treadmill so she could run.

After 90 minutes of exercise, it was time for the morning meeting. Magnus met with the ISS crew. They spoke on the radio with ground teams on Earth. Together, they planned out the day ahead. Then Magnus got to work.

Magnus was a flight engineer. This meant she would have many different tasks to do. Her first job was to test the station's water. Spacecraft deliver water to the station from Earth. But water is very heavy. Launching it to space is expensive. Being able to recycle water means that less needs to be brought to the ISS. A new water recycling system had recently been added. It collected water from sinks, showers, and the air. It made the water safe to drink. The astronauts had to frequently check the water. They needed to be sure the system was working right.

Next, Magnus floated over to one of the station's docking ports. A robotic supply ship had arrived recently. Now, its cargo had to be unloaded. Magnus moved boxes and bags from the supply ship into the station. It was difficult to find a place to put everything. The ISS is larger than a six-bedroom house. But it is crammed with supplies and equipment.

▲ **Magnus floats between two Russian space suits in December 2008.**

Magnus also spent time checking science experiments and making sure the ISS was working properly. Astronauts must frequently check the station's systems. Space is a dangerous place to live. Even a small problem could quickly become deadly.

After working all day, it was finally time for dinner with the other two astronauts on the crew. Food came in sealed packets.

Otherwise it might float away and damage the station. Magnus loved to eat tortillas in space. She could spread almost anything on them. That way, they could be eaten without making a mess.

With dinner finished, Magnus grabbed her camera. She floated over to a window that faced Earth. She began taking photos. Looking at the planet from space was amazing.

Finally, Magnus returned to her sleep pod. Magnus was looking forward to the next day on the station. As she fell asleep, she thought about the exciting five months on the ISS that were still ahead of her.

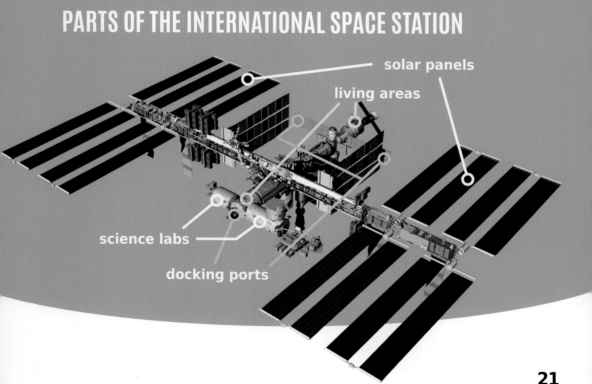

PARTS OF THE INTERNATIONAL SPACE STATION

solar panels

living areas

science labs

docking ports

GLOSSARY

cargo bay (KAR-go BAY): A cargo bay is the part of a space shuttle that holds large objects. The cargo bay has huge doors that open to space.

cosmonaut (KAHZ-muh-nawt): A cosmonaut is a Russian astronaut. The cosmonaut Sergei Krikalev helped build the ISS.

docking (DAH-king): Docking is the connecting together of two spacecraft. After docking, the space shuttle *Endeavour* was connected with the *Unity* module.

gravity (GRAV-i-tee): Gravity is the force that pulls things together. On the ISS, gravity does not pull objects to the floor.

module (MAH-jyool): A module is a piece of a space station. The mission was to connect the *Unity* module with the *Zarya* module.

orbit (OR-bit): An orbit is the circular or oval-shaped path an object takes around a star or planet. The ISS travels in an orbit around Earth.

solar panels (SOHL-ur PAN-ulz): Solar panels are devices that turn the sun's light into electricity. The ISS uses solar panels to power itself.

thrusters (THRUS-turz): Thrusters are small rockets that help a spacecraft change its speed or direction in space. The space shuttle *Endeavour* used its thrusters to meet with the *Zarya* module.

trusses (TRUS-ez): Trusses are structures that hold objects together. Trusses on the ISS join together the station's modules and solar panels.

SOURCE NOTES

1. David M. Harland and John E. Catchpole. *Creating the International Space Station*. New York: Springer, 2002. Print. 210.

2. Ines Hernandez. "Near Miss with Debris after ISS Crew Takes Shelter." *Space Safety Magazine*. Space Safety Magazine, 26 Mar. 2012. Web. 17 Jun. 2015.

TO LEARN MORE

Books

Baker, David, and Heather Kissock. *International Space Station*. New York: Weigl, 2009.

Etingoff, Kim. *ISS: The International Space Station*. Vestal, NY: Village Earth Press, 2014.

Nelson, Maria. *Life on the International Space Station*. New York: Gareth Stevens, 2013.

Web Sites

Visit our Web site for links about the International Space Station: childsworld.com/links

Note to Parents, Teachers, and Librarians: We routinely verify our Web links to make sure they are safe and active sites. So encourage your readers to check them out!

INDEX